THE WEALTH CODE

Insider Secrets from the World's Richest Individuals

WESLEY L. DIENER

Copyright © 2023 by Wesley L. Diener

Protected by copyright law.

No piece of this book might be utilized or replicated using any and all means, realistic, electronic, or mechanical, including copying, recording, taping, or by any data stockpiling recovery framework without the composed consent of the distributer with the exception of brief citations exemplified in basic articles and audits.

Table of Contents

Introduction: Unveiling the Wealth Code..................................pg 8

Part I: Laying the Foundation

Chapter 1: Understanding Wealth: Breaking Down the Myths..............................pg 13

1.1 Debunking common misconceptions about wealth accumulation

1.2 Exploring the true nature of wealth and its potential for everyone

1.3 Identifying the key drivers behind wealth creation

1.4 Understanding the role of mindset in attracting and maintaining wealth

Chapter 2: The Wealth Mindset: Cultivating a Prosperous Attitude....................pg 20

2.1 Shifting your mindset towards abundance and success

2.2 Embracing a growth mindset to overcome limiting beliefs

2.3 Developing resilience and persistence in the

pursuit of wealth

2.4 Harnessing the power of positive thinking and visualization

Chapter 3: Mastering Personal Finance: Building a Solid Financial Base................pg 25

3.1 The importance of budgeting, tracking expenses, and setting financial goals

3.2 Strategies for saving and investing to build wealth over time

3.3 Understanding the power of compound interest and long-term wealth growth

3.4 Managing debt effectively and leveraging it for wealth creation

Part II: Strategies of the Wealthy

Chapter 4: Wealthy Habits: Daily Routines for Financial Success...........................pg 31

4.1 Creating a morning routine to optimize productivity and focus

4.2 The power of goal setting and effective time management

4.3 Cultivating healthy habits for physical and mental well-being

4.4 Leveraging technology and automation to streamline financial processes

Chapter 5: The Power of Networking: Leveraging Connections for Wealth..........pg 41

5.1 Building a strong network of influential individuals

5.2 Strategies for cultivating meaningful relationships and connections

5.2 Leveraging social media and online platforms for networking

5.4 Creating mutually beneficial partnerships and collaborations

Chapter 6: Entrepreneurship and Wealth Creation: From Ideas to Profits...........pg 50

6.1 Identifying entrepreneurial opportunities and evaluating their potential

6.2 Navigating the challenges of starting and scaling a successful business

6.3 Building a solid business plan and executing it effectively

6.4 Harnessing innovation and adaptability to stay ahead in the market

Part III: Unlocking Secrets to Long-Term Wealth

Chapter 7: The Power of Passive Income: Generating Wealth While You Sleep..................................pg 58

7.1 Unveiling passive income streams and their potential for financial freedom

7.2 Creating passive income sources through investments, royalties, and licensing

7.3 Exploring digital entrepreneurship and online business models

7.4 Strategies for building multiple streams of passive income for wealth accumulation

Chapter 8: Wealth Preservation: Safeguarding and Growing Your Assets......................pg 64

8.1 Understanding asset protection strategies and risk management

8.2 Estate planning and wealth transfer to future generations

8.3 Investing in alternative assets and diversifying your portfolio

8.4 Maximizing tax efficiency and minimizing wealth erosion

Conclusion: Take-home Words ....pg 70

APPENDIX: Some Known World Richest Men and
How They Became Rich.............. Pg 74

INTRODUCTION

Unveiling the Wealth Code

Welcome, fellow adventurers, to the thrilling expedition into the realms of wealth and prosperity! As the author of "The Wealth Code: Insider Secrets from the World's Richest Individuals," I invite you to fasten your seatbelts and prepare for a mind-blowing journey of discovery. In this captivating book, we will unravel the enigmatic secrets that the world's wealthiest individuals have guarded for ages, waiting to be revealed to intrepid souls like yourself. So, grab your map, sharpen your wit, and let's embark on this exhilarating adventure together!

Picture this: a world where wealth is not an elusive dream or a distant mirage, but a tangible reality within your reach. We've all been captivated by the glamorous lives of the rich and famous, secretly wondering what it takes to walk in their designer shoes and bask in the glow of opulence. Well, my fellow treasure seekers, prepare to be astonished, because "The Wealth Code" will unveil the truth: wealth is not reserved for the lucky few or those born with silver spoons. It is a code, a set of principles and strategies that can be cracked and utilized by anyone daring enough to seize the opportunity.

Now, let's dive headfirst into the treasure chest of knowledge with our first piece of valuable loot: the power of mindset. It's time to do our mental armor and explore the captivating realm of prosperous thinking. Imagine a mindset that radiates abundance, shatters self-doubt, and opens doors to unimagined possibilities. By unleashing the force within and banishing the limiting beliefs that hold us back, we embark on a transformative journey towards greatness. Linking arms with a resilient mindset, we are equipped to conquer the challenges that await us on the path to wealth.

But wait, that's not all! Our map to riches leads us through treacherous terrain known as personal finance. Fear not, for I shall be your guide, helping you navigate the treacherous waters of budgeting, saving, and investing. We'll uncover the secrets of compound interest, learn to tame the beast of debt, and lay a solid financial foundation that will stand the test of time. With each step, we grow closer to unlocking the wealth that lies dormant within our grasp.

As we venture deeper into this thrilling expedition, we'll encounter extraordinary characters who have cracked the wealth code. These individuals have mastered the art of wealth creation through their daily habits, and we shall join their ranks. Prepare to be amazed as we discover the routines and rituals that fuel their success. From early morning rituals that ignite productivity to evening practices that foster relaxation and reflection, we'll learn the secrets to becoming masters of our own destiny.

Now, let's hoist our sails and navigate the stormy seas of networking. Brace yourselves, for the power of connections awaits. Together, we'll unravel the hidden magic that lies within our social web. By forging powerful alliances, we unlock a gateway to opportunities previously unimaginable. We'll explore the art of building fruitful relationships, leveraging technology to expand our networks, and discovering the transformative influence of collaboration. Are you ready to set sail on this voyage of connection?

Ahoy, fellow adventurers! We've reached the mysterious island known as entrepreneurship. Here, we'll unearth the treasures hidden within bold ideas and courageous pursuits. We'll navigate the turbulent waters of business creation, from inception to profitability, learning from the triumphs and tribulations of those who have walked this path before. Brace yourself for tales of innovation, risk-taking, and the audacity to dream big. Together, we'll unleash the entrepreneurial spirit that lies dormant within, transforming it into a force capable of generating untold wealth.

But hold onto your hats for the journey doesn't end

there. We'll dive headfirst into the labyrinthine realm of investments, where fortunes are made and lost. Fear not, for I shall equip you with the tools to navigate these perilous waters. We'll unravel the mysteries of stocks, bonds, real estate, and more, learning to read the signs, seize the opportunities, and make informed decisions. With each investment choice, we inch closer to untold riches.

As our adventure draws to a close, we shall unlock the final vault: the secrets of wealth preservation. Together, we'll safeguard our hard-earned treasures through prudent asset protection and risk management. We'll chart a course through the intricate waters of estate planning, uncover the hidden potential of alternative investments, and unleash the magic of tax optimization. Our wealth shall stand strong, impervious to the storms that may threaten to erode it.

So, my fellow Investors, as we stand on the precipice of this grand expedition, I implore you to embrace the unknown, challenge your limits, and embark on this exhilarating quest to unravel "The Wealth Code: Insider Secrets from the World's Richest Individuals." The treasures that lie ahead are not merely material riches but the keys to unlocking your full potential and living a life of abundance. So, strap on your explorer's hat, seize your copy of the book, and let's embark on this extraordinary adventure together!

CHAPTER 1

Understanding Wealth: Breaking Down the Myths

Welcome to the first chapter of our exhilarating journey through the world of wealth creation. In this chapter, we delve into the very essence of wealth, unraveling the misconceptions that have clouded our understanding and setting the stage for a transformative shift in perspective. So, buckle up and get ready to challenge everything you thought you knew about wealth.

Firstly, let's cast aside the illusions that have misled us for far too long. Wealth is not some elusive fantasy attainable only by the lucky few or those with a silver spoon in their mouths. No, my dear readers, it is time to debunk those common myths surrounding wealth accumulation. We will shine a light on the fallacies that have held us back, such as the belief that wealth is solely determined by luck or inherited privilege. By confronting these misconceptions head-on, we liberate ourselves from the self-imposed limitations that have hindered our own financial growth.

Throughout history, numerous misconceptions about wealth have prevailed, perpetuating myths that hinder our understanding of its true nature. Let us shed light on few of these misconceptions below and debunk them one by one, opening the doors to a clearer understanding of wealth and its attainability for all.

1: Wealth is solely determined by luck or inherited privilege.

This myth suggests that only a fortunate few are destined to acquire wealth, either through inheritance or sheer luck. However, this notion overlooks the countless individuals who have risen from humble beginnings to achieve immense wealth through hard work, strategic decision-making, and perseverance. While luck and privilege may play a role in some instances, they are not the sole determinants of wealth. By dispelling this myth, we empower ourselves to believe that wealth is within our grasp through dedicated effort and the right mindset.

2: Wealth is a finite resource, and for one person to gain, another must lose.

This misconception fosters a scarcity mindset, where individuals believe that wealth creation is a zero-sum game. In reality, wealth is not fixed, and there is an abundance of resources and opportunities available to all. The growth of one person's wealth does not necessitate the deprivation of others. Through innovation, entrepreneurship, and collaboration, we can expand the economic pie and create win-win situations that benefit multiple parties. Understanding this truth enables us to embrace a mindset of abundance, where everyone can prosper together.

3: Wealth is solely measured by material possessions and monetary wealth.

This narrow view of wealth reduces its definition to material possessions and financial status. However, true wealth encompasses much more than monetary value. It includes elements such as personal fulfillment, meaningful relationships, good health, and a sense of purpose. By broadening our understanding of wealth, we free ourselves from the relentless pursuit of material accumulation and shift our focus towards holistic prosperity and well-being.

4: Wealth comes easily and quickly, requiring minimal effort.

This myth perpetuates the notion that wealth can be acquired overnight with minimal effort or expertise. In reality, building sustainable wealth requires dedication, discipline, and a willingness to invest time and resources into our goals. It often involves overcoming challenges, taking calculated risks, and learning from failures along the way. By dispelling this misconception, we recognize that wealth creation is a long-term journey that demands consistent effort and a growth mindset.

In our quest to understand wealth, we must also recognize the interplay between external factors and internal mindset. It is not enough to simply have knowledge of financial strategies and tactics; we must align our thoughts, beliefs, and attitudes with the abundance we seek. Our mindset acts as a powerful magnet, attracting or repelling wealth based on the signals we emit to the universe.

By cultivating a positive and abundance-focused mindset, we become open to opportunities and possibilities that would otherwise pass us by. We start to see the world through a different lens, one that recognizes abundance and potential in every situation. This mindset shift allows us to spot hidden opportunities, tap into our creativity, and make decisions that align with our wealth-building goals.

Gratitude, an often overlooked aspect of wealth creation, plays a pivotal role in shaping our mindset. When we appreciate what we already have, we invite more abundance into our lives. By expressing gratitude for our current financial situation, no matter how modest, we activate a powerful force that attracts more wealth. Gratitude helps us shift our focus from lack to abundance, allowing us to approach wealth creation from a place of abundance consciousness.

Generosity, too, is an essential aspect of wealth mindset. As we cultivate a spirit of giving, we tap into the universal law of reciprocity. By sharing our resources, time, and expertise, we create a flow of abundance that returns to us manifold. Generosity expands our capacity to receive and sends a message to the universe that we are open to receiving even greater wealth.

Another crucial element of wealth mindset is the belief in our own growth and potential. Embracing a growth mindset means viewing challenges and setbacks as opportunities for learning and improvement. We understand that failure is not a reflection of our worth but a stepping stone on the path to success. By cultivating resilience, perseverance, and a willingness to adapt, we position ourselves for long-term wealth accumulation.

As we conclude this chapter, let us reflect on the profound insights we have gained. We have shattered the illusions surrounding wealth, recognizing that it is not a privilege reserved for a select few but an attainable goal for all. We have explored the true nature of wealth, encompassing financial abundance, health, relationships, and purpose. We have identified the key drivers behind wealth creation and understood the critical role of mindset in attracting and maintaining wealth.

Armed with this newfound knowledge, we are ready to embark on the next leg of our journey, building upon this foundation and unlocking the secrets that the world's wealthiest individuals have utilized to amass their fortunes. As we continue, we will delve deeper into the strategies, habits, and actions that propel us towards lasting wealth. So, my fellow adventurers, let us press onward, guided by the understanding that wealth is not only within our reach but also within our grasp. Together, we will unveil "The Wealth Code" and transform our lives in ways we never thought possible.

By addressing and dispelling these misconceptions, we lay the foundation for a deeper understanding of wealth and its attainability. Wealth is not a distant dream reserved for a select few, but a goal that can be pursued by anyone who is willing to embrace the principles, strategies, and mindset required for its achievement. By debunking these myths, we open ourselves up to the immense possibilities that await us on our journey towards financial abundance and personal fulfillment.

CHAPTER 2

The Wealth Mindset: Cultivating a Prosperous Attitude

2.1 Shifting your mindset towards abundance and success

Mindset cultivation encompasses recognizing the pivotal role our attitudes and beliefs play in our quest for wealth. Many investors invest with wrong mindsets. The mindset for school is not the same mindset for finance neither is it used in another field of endeavors. Every field of engagements require specific mindset to successfully operate within the spheres of such field. It is time to shift our mindset from scarcity to abundance, from a fear of lack to a belief in unlimited possibilities.

Embracing the abundance mindset means recognizing that the universe is abundant and there is enough wealth and opportunities for everyone. It involves letting go of the fear of scarcity and cultivating a mindset of abundance consciousness. We begin to see the world as a place of abundance, where opportunities abound and prosperity is within our reach. By shifting our focus from what we lack to what we have and what we can create, we open ourselves up to new possibilities and attract wealth into our lives.

2.2 Embracing a growth mindset to overcome limiting beliefs

To cultivate a wealth mindset, we must also embrace a growth mindset. This mindset is grounded in the belief that our abilities and intelligence can be developed through effort, learning, and perseverance. It requires us to let go of fixed notions about our capabilities and embrace the idea that we can continuously grow and improve.

By adopting a growth mindset, we overcome limiting beliefs that may have held us back from pursuing wealth. We understand that failures and setbacks are opportunities for learning and growth, rather than indicators of our worth or potential. We view challenges as stepping stones on the path to success and approach them with resilience and determination. With a growth mindset, we become open to acquiring new skills, seeking knowledge, and embracing new opportunities, ultimately propelling us forward on our wealth-building journey.

2.3 Developing resilience and persistence in the pursuit of wealth

The pursuit of wealth is not without its challenges. Therefore, developing resilience and persistence is crucial in navigating the inevitable obstacles and setbacks that we may encounter along the way.

Resilience allows us to bounce back from failures and setbacks, learning from them and adapting our approach. It is the ability to persevere in the face of adversity, maintaining focus on our goals and pushing through difficulties.

To cultivate resilience, we must develop a strong belief in ourselves and our ability to overcome challenges. We cultivate a mindset that views failures as temporary setbacks, not permanent defeats. We seek support from mentors, surround ourselves with like-minded individuals, and build a network of resilience. By developing resilience, we gain the strength to weather storms and stay committed to our wealth-building journey, even in the face of adversity.

2.4 Harnessing the power of positive thinking and visualization

Positive thinking is a powerful tool that can shape our reality and attract wealth into our lives. By cultivating positive thoughts and beliefs, we create a magnetic force that draws abundance towards us. Positive thinking involves shifting our focus to the possibilities and opportunities that exist, rather than dwelling on limitations or negative circumstances.

Visualization, coupled with positive thinking, allows us to create a clear mental picture of our desired wealth and success. We vividly imagine ourselves living the life we desire, feeling the emotions associated with that reality. By regularly visualizing our goals and desires, we program our subconscious mind to seek out opportunities and take inspired action towards their attainment.

Every Investor must first and foremost embrace the supposed mindset for financial success before venturing into financial investments. We have embraced the abundance mindset, shifting our perspective from scarcity to abundance, and adopting a growth mindset that propels us forward. We have understood the importance of resilience and persistence, developing the strength to overcome challenges. Lastly, we have harnessed the power of positive thinking and visualization to align our thoughts and emotions with our desired wealth and success.

As we integrate these principles into our lives, we begin to transform our mindset and approach to wealth. We become the architects of our own success, harnessing the power within us to manifest abundance and achieve our financial goals. With a cultivated wealth mindset, we are poised to embark on the subsequent chapters, where we will delve deeper into the strategies and actions required to turn our mindset into tangible wealth.

CHAPTER 3

Mastering Personal Finance: Building a Solid Financial Base

In "The Wealth Code: Insider Secrets from the World's Richest Individuals," Chapter 3 takes us on a transformative journey towards mastering personal finance and building a solid financial base. This chapter's significance lies in its ability to equip readers with the essential knowledge and strategies employed by the world's wealthiest individuals to amass and maintain their fortunes.

The chapter begins by delving into the intricacies of personal finance management, offering readers practical insights on how to take control of their financial situation. It covers topics such as budgeting, expense tracking, and the optimization of savings and investments. By implementing the proven techniques shared within this chapter, readers gain the necessary tools to align their financial habits with those of the wealthy, laying a strong foundation for long-term wealth creation.

Furthermore, this chapter reveals the insider secrets of wealth accumulation, providing readers with a deeper understanding of the principles that underpin financial success. Readers learn about the significance of leveraging, diversifying income streams, and making strategic financial decisions.

By incorporating these strategies into our own financial practices, readers gain valuable insights into the methods utilized by the world's richest individuals to effectively grow their wealth over time.

3.1 The importance of budgeting, tracking expenses, and setting financial goals

Budgeting, tracking expenses, and setting financial goals play fundamental roles in mastering personal finance and building a solid financial base. Budgeting provides individuals with a clear overview of their income and expenses, allowing them to allocate their resources effectively. It enables individuals to identify areas of overspending and make necessary adjustments to align their expenses with their financial goals. Tracking expenses helps individuals become more mindful of their spending habits, encouraging them to make conscious choices that contribute to their long-term financial well-being.

Setting financial goals is equally crucial as it provides individuals with a sense of direction and purpose. By defining specific and achievable goals, individuals can prioritize their financial decisions and allocate resources accordingly. Financial goals can include saving for a down payment on a house, starting a business, or achieving early retirement. With clear goals in mind, individuals can make informed choices and stay motivated on their wealth-building journey.

3.2 Strategies for saving and investing to build wealth over time

Strategies for saving and investing form the core pillars of building wealth over time. Saving is the foundation for financial stability and future opportunities. It involves setting aside a portion of income on a regular basis, creating a safety net and capital for investment. By adopting disciplined saving habits, individuals accumulate funds that can be utilized for various purposes, such as emergencies, education, or investment opportunities. Saving sets the stage for individuals to take advantage of potential wealth-building avenues.

Investing is the next step in the wealth-building process. It involves putting saved funds into assets that have the potential to grow and generate returns over time. Readers are introduced to a range of investment options, including stocks, bonds, real estate, and mutual funds. Diversification and risk management are emphasized to ensure a balanced and resilient investment portfolio. By understanding different investment strategies and their associated risks, individuals can make informed decisions that align with their risk tolerance and long-term financial goals.

3.3 Understanding the power of compound interest and long-term wealth growth

The power of compound interest is a key concept in understanding long-term wealth growth. Compound interest refers to earning interest not only on the initial investment but also on the accumulated interest over time. This compounding effect enables individuals to witness exponential growth in their investments. Understanding the mechanics of compound interest empowers readers to appreciate the significance of starting early and staying invested for extended periods.

By embracing a long-term perspective, individuals can benefit from the compounding effect, where even small, consistent contributions can lead to substantial wealth accumulation over time. The subtopic emphasizes the importance of patience and consistent saving and investing habits. By capitalizing on the power of compound interest, individuals can leverage time as an ally and amplify their wealth-building efforts.

By emphasizing budgeting, expense tracking, and setting financial goals, individuals lay the groundwork for making informed financial decisions. The strategies for saving and investing equip readers with the tools to grow their wealth steadily over time. Understanding the power of compound interest highlights the significance of a long-term perspective and consistent contributions. Together, these subtopics contribute to the overall goal of building a solid financial base and mastering personal finance for long-term wealth creation.

Part II: Strategies of the Wealthy

CHAPTER 4

Wealthy Habits: Daily Routines for Financial Success

Chapter 4, "Wealthy Habits: Daily Routines for Financial Success," makes a significant contribution to "The Wealth Code: Insider Secrets from the World's Richest Individuals." This chapter delves into the power of habits and routines in shaping financial success. By exploring the daily practices and rituals of the world's wealthiest individuals, readers gain valuable insights into the mindset and behaviors that have led to their financial prosperity.

The chapter emphasizes the idea that success leaves clues, and by adopting the habits of the wealthy, individuals can unlock the secrets to their financial achievements. It delves into various aspects of daily routines, such as morning rituals, goal setting, time management, and continuous learning. Readers are provided with practical strategies and techniques to incorporate into their own lives, enabling them to cultivate the habits necessary for financial success.

4.1 Creating a morning routine to optimize productivity and focus:

Having a structured morning routine is a key habit of successful individuals. In this subtopic, Chapter 4 explores the significance of starting the day with purpose and intention. By crafting a morning routine that aligns with personal goals and values, individuals can optimize their productivity and focus. This section delves into the various elements that can be incorporated into a morning routine, such as meditation, exercise, journaling, or reading. By establishing a consistent and empowering morning routine, individuals can set a positive tone for the day ahead and cultivate habits that promote long-term financial success.

A well-designed morning routine helps individuals seize control of their day right from the start. By waking up early and dedicating time to activities that align with their goals, individuals can create a sense of accomplishment and momentum. For example, incorporating mindfulness or meditation practices in the morning can promote mental clarity and reduce stress, allowing individuals to approach financial decisions with a calm and focused mindset. Additionally, engaging in physical exercise during the morning routine boosts energy levels and enhances cognitive function, setting the stage for improved productivity throughout the day.

Moreover, a morning routine provides an opportunity to establish healthy habits that contribute to overall well-being. By allocating time for self-care activities like reading, journaling, or gratitude exercises, individuals nurture their mental and emotional health. This, in turn, positively impacts their financial decision-making abilities. Through consistent practice, these habits become ingrained, leading to greater self-discipline and resilience. Over time, a morning routine becomes a powerful tool for building momentum, enhancing productivity, and cultivating the mindset necessary for financial success.

4.2 The power of goal setting and effective time management:

Goal setting and effective time management are crucial components of a wealthy individual's daily routine. This subtopic emphasizes the importance of setting clear and actionable financial goals. It explores techniques for breaking down larger goals into smaller, manageable tasks and prioritizing them effectively. By aligning daily activities with long-term objectives, individuals can make significant progress towards their financial aspirations. Additionally, this section delves into time management strategies, such as the Pomodoro Technique or time blocking, which help individuals maximize their productivity and ensure that their efforts are directed towards tasks that contribute to financial success.

Goal setting serves as a roadmap for achieving financial success. By setting specific, measurable, achievable, relevant, and time-bound (SMART) goals, individuals gain clarity on what they want to accomplish and by when. This clarity enables them to allocate their time and resources effectively.

4.3 Cultivating healthy habits for physical and mental well-being:

In order to achieve financial success, it is essential to prioritize physical and mental well-being. This subtopic highlights the importance of cultivating healthy habits to support overall wellness. It explores the benefits of regular exercise, proper nutrition, and sufficient sleep in maintaining peak performance and mental clarity. Additionally, this section delves into strategies for managing stress and promoting mindfulness, which are vital for making sound financial decisions. By nurturing physical and mental health, individuals can sustain the energy, focus, and resilience necessary for long-term financial success.

Physical and mental well-being are the foundation upon which financial success is built. The subtopic emphasizes the role of regular exercise in promoting physical health and enhancing cognitive function. Engaging in physical activities not only boosts energy levels but also improves focus, memory, and problem-solving abilities. By incorporating exercise into their daily routines, individuals can enhance their overall well-being and, consequently, their financial performance. This section explores different forms of exercise and provides guidance on finding a routine that suits individual preferences and lifestyles.

Proper nutrition is another crucial aspect of cultivating healthy habits. This subtopic delves into the importance of a balanced diet in supporting optimal physical and mental functioning. By fueling the body with nutritious foods, individuals can maintain stable energy levels and enhance brain function, leading to improved decision-making abilities. Furthermore, the subtopic highlights the significance of sufficient sleep in promoting well-being and reducing stress. Adequate rest and recovery enable individuals to recharge and rejuvenate, enhancing their overall productivity and resilience in the face of financial challenges.

Managing stress and promoting mindfulness are essential practices for maintaining mental well-being. The subtopic explores stress management techniques such as meditation, deep breathing exercises, and mindfulness practices. These techniques help individuals cultivate emotional resilience and reduce anxiety, which in turn allows for clearer thinking and better financial decision-making. By prioritizing mental health and incorporating stress management techniques into their daily routines, individuals can optimize their overall well-being and set the stage for long-term financial success.

4.4 Leveraging technology and automation to streamline financial processes:

In today's digital age, technology and automation have transformed the way we manage our finances. This subtopic highlights the power of leveraging technology to streamline financial processes, ultimately leading to greater efficiency and success. Chapter 4 explores various tools, platforms, and applications that can simplify tasks such as budgeting, expense tracking, and investment management. By adopting automated systems, individuals can save time, reduce human error, and gain a comprehensive view of their financial situation.

One of the key benefits of technology in financial management is the ability to automate routine tasks. For example, budgeting apps and software can automatically categorize expenses, generate spending reports, and provide real-time updates on financial progress. By integrating bank accounts and credit cards, these tools can streamline the process of tracking and analyzing financial transactions. Furthermore, automation allows for the setting of financial goals, providing reminders and notifications to help individuals stay on track and achieve their objectives. By eliminating manual data entry and calculations, technology enables individuals to focus more on strategic financial decisions.

Additionally, technology plays a crucial role in investment management. Online platforms and robo-advisors have emerged as convenient and cost-effective solutions for individuals seeking to invest their money. These platforms use algorithms and artificial intelligence to analyze market trends, assess risk profiles, and automatically allocate funds across a diversified portfolio. By leveraging technology, individuals can access investment opportunities, monitor performance, and make adjustments in a seamless and efficient manner. This reduces the need for extensive financial knowledge and active portfolio management, making investing more accessible to a wider range of individuals.

Moreover, technology-driven automation extends beyond basic financial tasks. It can streamline processes such as bill payments, account transfers, and tax calculations. Online banking platforms and financial management apps offer features that automate these tasks, ensuring accuracy, timeliness, and convenience. For example, scheduled payments and direct debits can be set up to handle regular bills, eliminating the need for manual intervention. Similarly, automated tax software can streamline the process of preparing and filing tax returns, reducing the likelihood of errors and ensuring compliance with tax regulations.

Chapter 4 explores the process of defining short-term and long-term financial goals and provides strategies for breaking them down into actionable steps. By breaking goals into smaller tasks, individuals can focus on one task at a time, making their objectives more attainable and manageable.

Effective time management is also vital for maximizing productivity and achieving financial goals. These techniques help individuals overcome procrastination, maintain focus, and allocate time efficiently. By mastering time management, individuals can prioritize tasks, minimize distractions, and make significant progress towards their financial objectives. Furthermore, effective time management also enables individuals to strike a healthy work-life balance, ensuring that personal and leisure activities are adequately incorporated into their daily routines.

CHAPTER 5

The Power of Networking: Leveraging Connections for Wealth

This chapter explores the critical role of networking in the pursuit of financial success and provides readers with actionable strategies to harness the power of connections. By delving into the secrets of successful individuals who have built extensive networks, readers gain valuable insights and practical advice on how to effectively network to propel their own wealth-building endeavors.

Emphasis is laid on the importance of developing genuine relationships based on trust and reciprocity. It highlights that networking is not merely about superficial connections but about cultivating meaningful associations that can open doors to new opportunities. By sharing inspiring stories and real-world examples, the chapter illustrates how the world's wealthiest individuals have harnessed the power of networking to accelerate their financial journeys. Readers learn how to approach networking with authenticity, actively listen to others, and provide value to their connections, ultimately creating a mutually beneficial ecosystem.

Furthermore, it explores the practical strategies for

expanding one's professional network, and provides guidance on identifying key individuals in relevant industries or fields and offers insights into effective networking events, conferences, and online platforms where connections can be fostered. Readers are encouraged to step out of their comfort zones, embrace opportunities for networking, and cultivate a growth-oriented mindset. The chapter emphasizes that networking is a long-term investment, requiring consistent effort and a willingness to build and nurture relationships over time.

5.1 Building a strong network of influential individuals:

Building a strong network of influential individuals is a deliberate and strategic process that requires a proactive approach. It involves identifying key individuals who have achieved remarkable success in your industry or desired field. Attending industry conferences, seminars, and networking events provides opportunities to connect with these influential individuals. To make meaningful connections, it's important to approach these interactions with a genuine interest in learning from their experiences and accomplishments. Engage in conversations that go beyond small talk by asking thoughtful questions and actively listening to their insights. Show genuine curiosity and demonstrate your eagerness to learn from their expertise. By positioning yourself as someone who is genuinely interested in their work and accomplishments, you can build a foundation for a meaningful relationship.

Additionally, it's crucial to be proactive in offering value to influential individuals. Consider ways in which you can contribute to their goals or projects. Whether it's sharing your own expertise, providing valuable insights, or offering assistance, these acts of contribution can help establish your credibility and create a lasting impression. Building a strong network of influential individuals is not about collecting a large number of superficial connections; it's about nurturing a select group of meaningful relationships that can provide invaluable guidance, mentorship, and access to exclusive opportunities. By investing time and effort into building these connections, you can leverage their knowledge and network to accelerate your own wealth-building journey.

5.2 Strategies for cultivating meaningful relationships and connections:

Cultivating meaningful relationships and connections is a multifaceted process that requires genuine effort and intention. It begins with active and empathetic listening, which allows you to understand the needs, challenges, and aspirations of others. By genuinely listening and showing empathy, you can establish a strong foundation for building rapport and trust. Engage in conversations that go beyond superficial topics and demonstrate a sincere interest in others' personal and professional lives. This deeper level of connection creates a sense of mutual understanding and fosters authentic relationships.

Consistency in communication is another critical aspect of cultivating meaningful relationships. Regularly staying in touch, whether through emails, phone calls, or in-person meetings, demonstrates your commitment to nurturing the connection. Follow up on previous conversations, acknowledge important milestones, and offer support when needed. Showing appreciation for others' contributions is also essential. Recognize and celebrate their successes, and be genuinely supportive during challenging times. By actively engaging and staying present in the lives of your connections, you build a reputation as someone who genuinely cares and values the relationship. Cultivating meaningful relationships goes beyond superficial networking; it involves investing time, attention, and care to build genuine connections that can yield long-term benefits in your wealth-building journey.

5.3 Leveraging social media and online platforms for networking:

In today's digital age, social media and online platforms offer vast opportunities for networking and expanding your connections. Start by optimizing your professional profiles on platforms such as LinkedIn, ensuring they effectively showcase your expertise, achievements, and aspirations. Actively engage with relevant communities and groups within your industry. Participate in discussions, share your insights, and offer valuable feedback to others' posts. By consistently contributing meaningful content, you position yourself as a thought leader in your field and attract like-minded individuals who resonate with your expertise.

Strategic engagement is key when leveraging social media and online platforms. Instead of simply broadcasting information, focus on building genuine relationships. Initiate conversations, ask thought-provoking questions, and offer support to others. Actively seek out opportunities to connect with influential individuals by engaging with their content and sharing valuable insights. Additionally, consider participating in virtual events and webinars that are relevant to your industry. These platforms provide opportunities to connect with industry leaders, experts, and potential collaborators from all over the world. By leveraging social media and online platforms effectively, you can expand your network beyond geographical boundaries, gain exposure to new ideas and perspectives, and access a wealth of knowledge and opportunities that contribute to your financial success.

5.4 Creating mutually beneficial partnerships and collaborations:

Creating mutually beneficial partnerships and collaborations is a powerful strategy for leveraging connections to create wealth. Instead of viewing others as competitors, consider identifying individuals or organizations whose strengths and resources complement your own. Look for shared goals and objectives that can be achieved more effectively through collaboration rather than working alone. These partnerships can take various forms, such as joint projects, co-marketing efforts, or even co-creating products or services.

To create successful partnerships, it's important to conduct thorough research and due diligence. Identify potential partners who have a track record of success, align with your values, and possess expertise that complements yours. When approaching potential partners, articulate the value you bring to the table and how a collaboration can mutually enhance both parties' outcomes. Clearly define roles and responsibilities, set expectations, and establish open lines of communication to ensure a smooth and productive partnership.

Mutually beneficial partnerships offer numerous benefits. By pooling expertise and resources, you can access new markets, expand your customer base, and tap into additional knowledge and skills that can accelerate your wealth-building efforts. Collaborative ventures can also lead to increased credibility and visibility as you leverage each other's networks and leverage the collective power of your combined reputations.

Nurturing these partnerships is essential for long-term success. Regularly communicate, share updates, and provide support to your partners. By maintaining a strong and collaborative relationship, you can explore new opportunities, adapt to changing market dynamics, and continue to innovate together.

By leveraging the power of mutually beneficial partnerships and collaborations, you can amplify your wealth-building efforts, access new avenues for growth, and achieve greater success than what you could have accomplished alone.

Overall, Chapter 5: "The Power of Networking: Leveraging Connections for Wealth" explores various subtopics that contribute to a comprehensive understanding of networking's role in financial success. By addressing the importance of building influential networks, cultivating meaningful relationships, leveraging online platforms, and creating mutually beneficial partnerships, this chapter equips readers with the tools, strategies, and mindset required to harness the power of connections. Through these subtopics, readers gain actionable insights to develop a strong network, establish meaningful relationships, leverage online platforms, and engage in collaborative efforts that can significantly impact their wealth-building journey.

CHAPTER 6

Entrepreneurship and Wealth Creation: From Ideas to Profits

Entrepreneurship plays a pivotal role in "The Wealth Code: Insider Secrets from the World's Richest Individuals," as it unveils the path from generating ideas to turning them into profitable ventures. This chapter delves into the strategies and insights employed by the world's wealthiest individuals to build successful businesses and create substantial wealth. It begins by guiding readers in identifying entrepreneurial opportunities and evaluating their potential, emphasizing the importance of market research, innovation, and understanding consumer needs. Drawing from the experiences of renowned entrepreneurs, the chapter provides practical advice on developing a solid business plan, securing funding, and executing it effectively.

Furthermore, "The Wealth Code" explores the challenges inherent in entrepreneurship and offers solutions for overcoming them. It discusses the significance of adaptability, resilience, and a growth mindset in navigating the ever-changing business landscape. Readers are introduced to the concept of scaling a business, understanding how to expand operations while maintaining profitability. The chapter also emphasizes the importance of building a strong team and leveraging partnerships and collaborations to accelerate growth. With a focus on real-world examples and case studies, this chapter equips readers with the necessary tools and knowledge to embark on their entrepreneurial journey and unlock the potential for wealth creation through business ownership.

6.1 Identifying entrepreneurial opportunities and evaluating their potential:

In today's global market, identifying entrepreneurial opportunities requires a keen understanding of industry trends and consumer needs. Successful entrepreneurs have a knack for spotting gaps in the market and leveraging them to their advantage. They stay attuned to emerging industries, disruptive technologies, and evolving consumer behaviors. By conducting thorough market research and analysis, entrepreneurs can identify untapped niches, underserved markets, and opportunities for innovation. They study competitors, evaluate market demand, and assess the potential profitability of their ideas. This allows them to make informed choices about which opportunities to pursue, ensuring that their entrepreneurial endeavors have a strong foundation for success.

Entrepreneurs who excel in evaluating potential opportunities possess a combination of analytical thinking and creativity. They leverage data-driven decision-making, analyzing market trends, consumer preferences, and industry dynamics to identify viable business prospects. By identifying gaps in the market or pain points experienced by consumers, entrepreneurs can develop unique solutions that differentiate them from competitors. They also consider the scalability and sustainability of their ideas, ensuring that their ventures have long-term growth potential. Through careful evaluation and strategic thinking, successful entrepreneurs can identify the most promising opportunities and focus their efforts on ventures that have the greatest potential for wealth creation.

6.2 Navigating the challenges of starting and scaling a successful business:

Starting and scaling a successful business is a challenging endeavor that requires entrepreneurs to navigate various obstacles. In the global market, securing adequate funding is often a key challenge faced by entrepreneurs. They explore different financing options, such as angel investors, venture capital, crowdfunding, or bootstrapping, to fund their ventures. Successful entrepreneurs also recognize the importance of effectively managing cash flow to ensure the sustainability of their businesses. They develop financial strategies to optimize revenue generation, minimize expenses, and maintain a healthy financial position.

As entrepreneurs progress in their journey, scaling the business becomes a crucial goal. This involves expanding operations while maintaining quality and profitability. Entrepreneurs establish scalable systems and processes to handle increased demand and effectively manage growth. They focus on building a talented team, delegating tasks, and fostering a positive work culture to ensure operational efficiency. Successful entrepreneurs continuously seek ways to improve their business models, seeking feedback from customers and adapting to changing market conditions. They anticipate challenges and pivot their strategies when needed, embracing innovation and adaptability as key drivers of success. By effectively navigating the challenges of starting and scaling a business, entrepreneurs lay the foundation for long-term wealth creation and sustainable growth.

6.3 Building a solid business plan and executing it effectively:

In the global market, a well-crafted business plan is essential for entrepreneurs to attract investors, secure funding, and guide their operations. Successful entrepreneurs understand the importance of developing a solid business plan that serves as a roadmap for their venture. They meticulously outline their vision, mission, and goals, ensuring clarity and alignment across the organization. Through comprehensive market research, entrepreneurs identify their target audience, understand their needs, and position their products or services accordingly. They conduct a competitive analysis to identify their unique value proposition and differentiate themselves in the market.

A solid business plan includes actionable strategies and specific objectives. Entrepreneurs outline their marketing and sales strategies, identifying channels and tactics to reach their target market effectively. They develop financial projections, including revenue forecasts, expense budgets, and cash flow projections. Additionally, entrepreneurs create operational frameworks, defining key processes, roles, and responsibilities within their organizations. By building a solid business plan, entrepreneurs gain a clear understanding of their business landscape, mitigate risks, and lay the foundation for successful execution.

6.4 Harnessing innovation and adaptability to stay ahead in the market:

In the dynamic global market, innovation and adaptability are paramount for entrepreneurs aiming to achieve long-term success and wealth creation. Successful entrepreneurs foster a culture of innovation within their organizations, encouraging creativity and embracing new ideas. They stay updated on industry trends, technological advancements, and shifting consumer preferences. By leveraging market insights, they identify opportunities to innovate their products, services, or business models to stay ahead of the competition.

Entrepreneurs understand that adaptability is key to navigating the ever-changing business landscape. They proactively monitor market shifts, anticipate challenges, and adjust their strategies accordingly. This includes being open to feedback, seeking customer input, and making iterative improvements to their offerings. Successful entrepreneurs also emphasize continuous learning and personal development. They invest in their own growth, stay informed about industry developments, and acquire new skills to adapt to emerging trends. By harnessing innovation and adaptability, entrepreneurs position themselves as industry leaders, seize new opportunities, and sustain their competitive advantage, ultimately driving wealth creation in the global market.

Part III: Unlocking Secrets to Long-Term Wealth

CHAPTER 7

The Power of Passive Income: Generating Wealth While You Sleep

Passive income is a key concept explored in "The Wealth Code: Insider Secrets from the World's Richest Individuals." This chapter delves into the transformative potential of generating income streams that continue to grow and accumulate even when you're not actively working. It uncovers the secrets behind building sustainable passive income sources that contribute to long-term wealth creation.

This chapter reveals proven strategies and insights used by the world's wealthiest individuals to generate income while enjoying the freedom to pursue other endeavors. It explores various avenues for creating passive income, such as investments, royalties, and licensing. Readers gain a deep understanding of how to leverage these opportunities, including digital entrepreneurship and online business models, to build multiple streams of passive income. The chapter also emphasizes the importance of diversification and provides practical guidance on optimizing tax efficiency to preserve and grow wealth over time. By embracing the power of passive income, readers can unlock a significant pathway towards financial independence and achieve a level of prosperity enjoyed by the world's richest individuals.

7.1 Unveiling passive income streams and their potential for financial freedom:

Passive income streams have emerged as powerful tools for achieving financial freedom in the global economy. In today's interconnected world, individuals have access to a wide range of passive income opportunities that can generate consistent earnings without requiring constant active involvement. These streams can include rental properties, dividends from stocks, interest from bonds, and royalties from creative works. By diversifying income sources and leveraging these passive streams, individuals can break free from the limitations of traditional employment and enjoy greater financial flexibility. The potential for financial freedom lies in the ability to generate ongoing income that continues to flow even when one is not actively working, providing a sense of security and allowing for more time and resources to pursue personal goals and aspirations.

7.2 Creating passive income sources through investments, royalties, and licensing:

Creating passive income sources through investments, royalties, and licensing has become increasingly prevalent in the global economy. Investments offer opportunities for individuals to earn passive income through the growth and appreciation of assets. This can include investing in stocks, bonds, real estate, or even venture capital funds. Royalties from intellectual property, such as books, music, or patents, can provide a continuous stream of income for creators. Licensing intellectual property rights to businesses for commercial use is another way to generate passive income. By leveraging these avenues, individuals can tap into the global marketplace and create passive income streams that are not bound by geographical constraints. This diversification of income sources helps mitigate risks and provides the potential for substantial wealth accumulation over time, contributing to financial security and freedom.

7.3 Exploring digital entrepreneurship and online business models:

The advent of the digital age has revolutionized the way individuals can generate passive income in the global economy. Digital entrepreneurship and online business models have opened up a world of opportunities for individuals to create scalable and automated income streams. The internet provides a vast marketplace accessible to anyone with an internet connection, enabling entrepreneurs to reach a global audience. Online business models such as e-commerce stores, affiliate marketing, dropshipping, and digital products offer avenues for passive income generation. By harnessing the power of digital marketing, social media platforms, and automation tools, individuals can optimize their online businesses for success and create passive income streams that continue to generate revenue while they focus on other aspects of their lives. Exploring these digital entrepreneurship opportunities empowers individuals to leverage the global economy and tap into the immense potential for passive income generation.

7.4 Strategies for building multiple streams of passive income for wealth accumulation:

Building multiple streams of passive income has become a crucial strategy for wealth accumulation in the global economy. Relying on a single income source can be risky, as economic shifts and market fluctuations can disrupt earnings. To mitigate this risk and create a resilient financial portfolio, individuals should focus on diversifying their passive income streams. This can involve a combination of different investment vehicles, such as stocks, bonds, real estate, and peer-to-peer lending platforms. Additionally, exploring various passive income sources, such as rental properties, royalties, licensing agreements, and online business ventures, can provide additional streams of income. By strategically building multiple passive income streams, individuals can increase their earning potential, protect against volatility, and create a solid foundation for long-term wealth accumulation. This approach ensures financial security and opens up opportunities for individuals to achieve their financial goals and aspirations.

CHAPTER 8

Wealth Preservation: Safeguarding and Growing Your Assets

In today's global economy, wealth preservation has become a crucial aspect of financial planning for individuals seeking to safeguard and grow their assets. As economic landscapes continually evolve and financial uncertainties arise, it is essential to implement effective strategies to protect one's wealth from potential risks and ensure its long-term growth. Wealth preservation encompasses various practices and considerations, including asset protection, estate planning, diversification, and tax optimization.

One key aspect of wealth preservation is asset protection. In an interconnected and volatile global economy, individuals must adopt measures to shield their assets from potential risks such as lawsuits, economic downturns, or unexpected events. This involves utilizing legal and financial mechanisms to safeguard assets, such as establishing trusts, forming corporations, and obtaining appropriate insurance coverage. By implementing these strategies, individuals can mitigate potential threats and maintain the value of their wealth.

Additionally, wealth preservation involves

comprehensive estate planning to ensure the smooth transfer of assets to future generations. Through proper estate planning, individuals can minimize taxes, protect family legacies, and distribute their wealth according to their wishes. This may involve creating wills, establishing trusts, and utilizing gifting strategies to optimize tax efficiency and provide for heirs. Furthermore, diversifying investments across various asset classes and geographic regions can help mitigate risk and maximize long-term returns. By carefully considering these factors and staying informed about evolving economic trends, individuals can successfully navigate the global economy and secure the preservation and growth of their wealth.

8.1 Understanding asset protection strategies and risk management in the global economy:

In the global economy, understanding asset protection strategies and implementing effective risk management techniques are crucial for preserving and growing wealth. As individuals accumulate assets across borders and engage in international business ventures, they face a multitude of risks, including legal, economic, and geopolitical uncertainties. Implementing asset protection strategies involves identifying potential risks and taking proactive measures to shield assets from those risks. This may involve creating offshore structures, utilizing international trusts, or diversifying ownership across jurisdictions. Additionally, risk management techniques, such as insurance coverage and hedging strategies, can help mitigate potential financial losses due to unforeseen events or market fluctuations. By understanding these strategies and adopting a proactive approach, individuals can safeguard their assets and navigate the complexities of the global economy with greater confidence.

8.2 Estate planning and wealth transfer to future generations in the global economy:

Estate planning and wealth transfer in the global economy present unique challenges and opportunities. With wealth often distributed across multiple countries and jurisdictions, individuals must navigate complex legal and tax systems to ensure a smooth transfer of assets to future generations. International estate planning involves structuring assets in a way that minimizes tax liabilities, complies with applicable laws, and addresses cross-border complexities. This may include establishing trusts, utilizing tax-efficient vehicles, and implementing strategies to protect family legacies. Furthermore, individuals with global assets must consider the impact of different legal systems and cultural norms on inheritance laws and succession planning. By engaging in comprehensive estate planning and seeking professional guidance, individuals can optimize wealth transfer, minimize disputes, and secure their legacies across the global economy.

8.3 Investing in alternative assets and diversifying your portfolio in the global economy:

In the global economy, investing in alternative assets and diversifying one's portfolio has gained significance as individuals seek to maximize returns and manage risk. Traditional investment options may not always provide the desired level of diversification or attractive risk-adjusted returns. Alternative assets, such as private equity, venture capital, real estate, commodities, and cryptocurrencies, offer opportunities for diversification and potential for higher returns. These assets often have lower correlation with traditional markets, providing a hedge against volatility and economic downturns. Moreover, investing in alternative assets can help individuals tap into emerging markets and industries, capturing growth opportunities on a global scale. By incorporating alternative assets into their investment portfolios, individuals can enhance their chances of wealth accumulation and navigate the evolving dynamics of the global economy.

8.4 Maximizing tax efficiency and minimizing wealth erosion in the global economy:

In the global economy, maximizing tax efficiency and minimizing wealth erosion are vital considerations for individuals aiming to preserve and grow their assets. With varying tax systems and regulations across different jurisdictions, individuals must navigate complex tax landscapes to optimize their tax positions. This may involve utilizing tax-efficient structures, such as trusts, holding companies, or international tax treaties, to minimize tax liabilities and enhance wealth preservation. Additionally, individuals must stay informed about tax planning opportunities, such as deductions, exemptions, and incentives, that may be available in different countries. By adopting effective tax planning strategies, individuals can ensure that their wealth is not eroded by excessive tax burdens, thereby preserving more of their assets for future growth and financial security in the global economy.

CONCLUSION

Take-home Words

"The Wealth Code: Insider Secrets from the World's Richest Individuals" has taken us on a profound and comprehensive journey, illuminating the path to financial success by unveiling the strategies and wisdom employed by the world's wealthiest individuals. As we conclude this transformative exploration, we are equipped with a wealth of knowledge and tools to unlock our own potential and achieve prosperity. However, it is essential to approach the pursuit of wealth with caution and heed certain words of wisdom.

First and foremost, we must remember that wealth is not an overnight phenomenon. It requires persistence, discipline, and a long-term perspective. It is crucial to resist the allure of get-rich-quick schemes or shortcuts that promise instant wealth. Instead, we should focus on developing sound financial habits, making informed investment decisions, and consistently nurturing our financial growth over time.

Furthermore, we must be cautious of the risks and uncertainties inherent in the pursuit of wealth. Financial markets can be volatile, and economic conditions can change rapidly. It is vital to conduct thorough research, seek professional advice when needed, and diversify our investments to mitigate risk. Additionally, maintaining a prudent approach to debt management and avoiding excessive leverage is essential to safeguard our financial well-being.

While the insights shared in this book provide valuable guidance, it is crucial to adapt them to our own unique circumstances and risk tolerance. What works for one individual may not work for another. We must exercise discernment and tailor our financial strategies to align with our goals, values, and personal circumstances.

Moreover, we should remain vigilant and cautious of potential scams and fraudulent investment schemes that prey on the aspirations of individuals seeking wealth. Unfortunately, the allure of quick riches can attract unscrupulous individuals who exploit the unsuspecting. We must exercise due diligence, verify the credibility of investment opportunities, and be wary of promises that seem too good to be true.

As we embark on our own wealth-building journey, it is important to maintain a balanced perspective on wealth and its purpose. True wealth extends beyond material possessions. It encompasses aspects such as personal growth, meaningful relationships, and contributing to the greater good. Striving for wealth should be accompanied by a sense of responsibility and a commitment to using our resources to make a positive impact on the world around us.

Finally, let us remember that wealth is not an end in itself but a means to achieve our aspirations and live a fulfilling life. It is essential to strike a harmonious balance between the pursuit of financial success and other dimensions of our lives, such as health, relationships, and personal well-being. True wealth encompasses holistic prosperity and encompasses a well-rounded and meaningful existence.

Armed with the insights and strategies shared within "The Wealth Code," we are poised to embark on a journey of financial growth and prosperity. However, we must approach this pursuit with caution, heed words of wisdom, and adapt the principles to our unique circumstances. By doing so, we can navigate the complexities of wealth accumulation, mitigate risks, and strive for a well-rounded and purposeful life that extends far beyond material abundance.

APPENDIX

Some Known World Richest Men and How They Became Rich.

1. Elon Musk:

Elon Musk, the current richest person in the world, was born in South Africa and attended a Canadian university before transferring to the University of Pennsylvania, where he earned bachelor's degrees in physics and economics. Shortly after enrolling in a graduate physics program at Stanford University, Musk deferred his attendance to launch Zip2, an early online navigation service. He then used some of the proceeds from Zip2 to create X.com, an online payment system that eventually became PayPal Holdings after being sold to eBay (EBAY).

In 2004, Musk became a significant investor in Tesla Motors (now Tesla) and is now the CEO of the electric vehicle company. Tesla not only produces electric automobiles but also energy storage devices, automobile accessories, and solar power systems through its acquisition of

SolarCity in 2016. Musk also holds the positions of CEO and chief engineer at SpaceX, a company focused on developing space launch rockets.

In December 2020, Tesla joined the S&P 500, becoming the largest company added, and in January 2021, Musk became the richest person in the world, a title that has fluctuated with the value of Tesla.

In April 2022, Musk announced a campaign to take Twitter private through a $44 billion buyout, planning to fund the deal with $21 billion of his own capital. Prior to the buyout announcement, Musk sold 9.6 million shares of Tesla valued at approximately $8.5 billion.

In July 2022, Musk initially backed out of the Twitter buyout, leading to a lawsuit filed against him by Twitter. Musk later countersued the company but eventually declared his willingness to proceed with the buyout. The deal was officially closed in October 2022, giving Musk a 79% stake in Twitter.

2. Bernard Arnault:

Bernard Arnault, a French national, serves as

the chair and CEO of LVMH, the world's largest luxury goods company. LVMH owns renowned brands such as Louis Vuitton, Hennessey, Marc Jacobs, and Sephora.

Arnault's wealth primarily comes from his substantial stake in Christian Dior SE, the holding company that controls 41.4% of LVMH. Through his family-owned holding company, Groupe Familial Arnault, he also holds an additional 6.2% stake in LVMH.

Starting as an engineer, Arnault demonstrated his business acumen while working for his father's construction firm, Ferret-Savinel. In 1971, he took over the company, which he later transformed into a real estate company named Férinel Inc. In 1984, Arnault acquired and reorganized luxury goods maker Financière Agache, eventually selling all its holdings except Christian Dior and Le Bon Marché. He was invited to invest in LVMH in 1987 and became the majority shareholder, chair of the board, and CEO of the company two years later.

3. Jeff Bezos:

In 1994, Jeff Bezos founded Amazon.com in a

Seattle garage shortly after leaving his position at the hedge fund giant D.E. Shaw. Initially pitching the idea of an online bookstore to his former boss, David E. Shaw, Bezos was met with disinterest.

While Amazon initially focused on selling books, it has since expanded into a comprehensive online marketplace offering a wide range of products. It is projected to surpass Walmart as the world's largest retailer by 2024. Amazon's diversification efforts include the acquisition of Whole Foods in 2017 and entry into the pharmacy business the same year.

Bezos owned up to 16% of Amazon in 2019 before transferring 4% to his former wife, MacKenzie Scott, during their divorce proceedings. In 2020, Amazon's share price jumped 76% on the heightened demand for online shopping amid the COVID-19 pandemic. On July 5, 2021, Jeff Bezos stepped down as CEO of Amazon and transitioned to the role of Executive Chairman. He has remained a significant shareholder in the company and continues to have a strong influence on its direction and strategy.

Apart from his involvement with Amazon, Bezos has pursued various other ventures. In 2000, he founded Blue Origin, a private aerospace manufacturer and spaceflight services company. Blue Origin aims to make space travel more accessible and is actively working on developing reusable rockets and spacecraft.

Bezos is also known for his philanthropic endeavors. In 2018, he announced the creation of the Bezos Day One Fund, committing $2 billion to address homelessness and establish high-quality preschools in low-income communities. Additionally, in 2020, he launched the Bezos Earth Fund with a $10 billion commitment to combat climate change.

4. Bill Gates:

Bill Gates co-founded Microsoft Corporation in 1975, along with Paul Allen. Microsoft became one of the world's largest and most successful technology companies, primarily known for its operating systems and software products such as Microsoft Office.

Gates played a pivotal role in the development

of the personal computer industry, leading Microsoft to dominate the software market. He served as CEO of Microsoft until 2000 and as Chairman and Chief Software Architect until 2014. During his tenure, Gates focused on shaping the company's strategic direction and promoting its products globally.

In recent years, Gates has dedicated more of his time to philanthropy. Along with his ex-wife, Melinda Gates, he established the Bill & Melinda Gates Foundation in 2000, which has become one of the world's largest charitable organizations. The foundation focuses on addressing global health issues, reducing poverty, and improving education.

In May 2021, Bill and Melinda Gates announced their decision to end their marriage after 27 years but expressed their commitment to continuing their philanthropic work together.

5. Larry Ellison:

Larry Ellison is an American businessman and co-founder of Oracle Corporation, one of the world's leading enterprise software companies. Ellison served as the CEO of Oracle for several decades before stepping down in 2014. Under his leadership, Oracle became a dominant force in the database management and enterprise software market.

Ellison is known for his competitive nature and bold vision. He played a key role in transforming Oracle into a global technology powerhouse through strategic acquisitions and innovative product development. Ellison's leadership helped Oracle thrive in the highly competitive business software industry.

Aside from his work at Oracle, Ellison is also recognized for his passion for yacht racing. He has participated in and sponsored various high-profile sailing competitions, including the America's Cup.

6. Steve Ballmer:

Steve Ballmer is an American businessman who served as the CEO of Microsoft Corporation from 2000 to 2014. He joined Microsoft in 1980 as the company's 30th employee and played a crucial role in its early growth and success.

During his tenure as CEO, Ballmer focused on

expanding Microsoft's product portfolio and driving innovation across multiple business segments. Under his leadership, Microsoft launched major products such as Windows XP, Windows 7, and the Microsoft Office suite.

Ballmer was known for his energetic and passionate style of leadership. He played a pivotal role in shaping Microsoft's corporate culture and maintaining its position as one of the world's leading technology companies.

After leaving Microsoft, Ballmer has focused on philanthropy and civic engagement. He has been involved in various charitable activities and initiatives, including data-driven projects aimed at improving public policy and government efficiency.

7. Warren Buffett:

Warren Buffett is an American investor, business tycoon, and philanthropist. He is widely regarded as one of the most successful investors in history and has amassed a considerable fortune through his company Berkshire Hathaway.

Buffett is known for his long-term investment

approach and value investing principles. He has consistently demonstrated a keen eye for identifying undervalued companies with strong growth potential. Buffett has made notable investments in companies such as Coca-Cola, American Express, and Apple.

In addition to his investment activities, Buffett has pledged to give away the majority of his wealth to philanthropic causes. He teamed up with Bill and Melinda Gates in 2010 to launch the Giving Pledge, an initiative that encourages billionaires to commit a significant portion of their wealth to charitable endeavors.

8. Larry Page:

Larry Page is an American computer scientist and entrepreneur who co-founded Google Inc. alongside Sergey Brin in 1998. Google started as a research project at Stanford University and rapidly grew into the world's most widely used search engine and a global technology conglomerate under Page's leadership.

Page served as the CEO of Google from 1998 to 2001, and again from 2011 to 2015 when he became the CEO of Google's parent company,

Alphabet Inc. As CEO, he played a crucial role in guiding Google's strategic direction and overseeing its expansion into various product areas beyond search, including Google Maps, Google Chrome, and Android.

Page has been a strong advocate for innovation and has invested in numerous ventures outside of Google. He is known for his interest in emerging technologies, such as autonomous vehicles and clean energy solutions.

In December 2019, Page and Brin announced that they would step down from their executive roles at Alphabet, but they continue to hold significant influence as major shareholders.

9. Sergey Brin:

Sergey Brin is a Russian-born American computer scientist and entrepreneur. He co-founded Google Inc. with Larry Page and played a vital role in developing the company's search engine technology and overall strategy.

Brin served as the President of Google's parent company, Alphabet Inc., from 2015 to 2019. During his time at Google, he focused on key areas such as search, advertising, and Google X, the company's division responsible for innovative projects like self-driving cars and Google Glass.

Brin has been recognized for his contributions to the field of technology and has received numerous awards for his entrepreneurial achievements. He has also been involved in various philanthropic initiatives, including the establishment of the Brin Wojcicki Foundation, which supports charitable causes related to health and education.

10. Mark Zuckerberg:

Mark Zuckerberg, as mentioned earlier, is an American entrepreneur who co-founded Facebook in 2004 and has been instrumental in its growth and success. He served as the CEO of Facebook and played a significant role in shaping the company's mission and vision.

Under Zuckerberg's leadership, Facebook has expanded its user base to billions of people worldwide and has become a platform for connecting individuals, sharing content, and facilitating online communities. Despite facing challenges related to privacy concerns and misinformation, Facebook remains one of the most influential social media platforms globally.

Zuckerberg has also been involved in various philanthropic efforts. In addition to the Chan Zuckerberg Initiative, which he established with his wife Priscilla Chan, he has made significant donations to causes such as education and medical research.

These individuals have made substantial contributions to their respective industries and have had a profound impact on technology, finance, and philanthropy.

Some Pieces of Advice

If you want to get a little closer to making the richest billionaires rankings, you might need to become a technological innovator or luxury retail mastermind. Or you could keep it simple and focus on value investing.

It also wouldn't hurt to have been born into wealth; however, the greatest fortunes on this list started as good ideas that people with creativity, drive, and connections used to build some of the world's largest companies.

Starting out in the financial system can be both exciting and daunting. It's a journey that requires knowledge, discipline, and careful planning. Whether you're just beginning your career or looking to gain control of your personal finances, the following advice will help you navigate the world of money management and set a strong foundation for your financial future.

Education is key. Take the time to learn about personal finance, investment strategies, and basic financial concepts. There are numerous resources available, including books, seminars, and reputable online platforms, that can enhance your financial literacy. The more you know, the better equipped you'll be to make informed decisions and avoid common pitfalls.

Setting clear financial goals is crucial. Define both short-term and long-term objectives that align with your aspirations. Whether it's saving for a down payment, paying off debt, or building a retirement fund, having well-defined goals will help you stay focused and motivated throughout your financial journey.

Creating a budget is essential. Develop a budget to track your income and expenses. This will provide a clear picture of where your money is going and allow you to make necessary adjustments to align your spending with your financial goals. A budget will also help you identify areas where you can cut back and save more effectively.

Building an emergency fund is a priority. Start saving for emergencies as early as possible. Aim to have three to six months' worth of living expenses in a readily accessible account. An emergency fund provides a financial safety net and helps you avoid going into debt during unexpected situations.

Pay off high-interest debt. If you have high-interest debt, such as credit card debt, prioritize paying it off. High-interest debt can hinder your financial progress, so focus on eliminating it to save on interest payments and improve your overall financial health. Consider strategies like the debt snowball or debt avalanche method to accelerate your debt repayment.

Start investing early. Begin investing as early as

you can, even if it's with small amounts. Take advantage of compounding returns over time to grow your wealth. Consider options like low-cost index funds or exchange-traded funds (ETFs) for a diversified investment approach. Starting early gives your investments more time to grow.

Diversify your investments. Don't put all your eggs in one basket. Spread your investment portfolio across different asset classes and sectors to reduce risk. Diversification helps protect your investments from market fluctuations and can improve your chances of achieving long-term growth.

Save for retirement. Start saving for retirement early and take advantage of tax-advantaged retirement accounts, such as a 401(k) or Individual Retirement Account (IRA). Contribute consistently and consider increasing your contributions whenever possible to secure your financial future. The power of compounding and tax benefits can make a significant difference over time.

Monitor your credit. Keep a close eye on your credit score and report. Regularly review your credit report for accuracy and take steps to improve your credit score if necessary. A good credit score can positively impact your ability to secure loans and favorable interest rates, saving you money in the long run.

Consider seeking professional advice. Consulting with a financial advisor can provide personalized guidance based on your unique financial situation and goals. A professional can help you create a comprehensive financial plan, address any specific concerns, and offer valuable insights to optimize your financial strategy.

Building financial stability takes time and discipline. By educating yourself, setting clear goals, budgeting, saving for emergencies, paying off debt, investing wisely, and seeking professional advice when needed, you

can set yourself up for long-term financial success. Remember, each step you take towards financial empowerment brings you closer to a future of financial freedom and security.

www.ingramcontent.com/pod-product-compliance
Lightning Source LLC
Chambersburg PA
CBHW070122230526
45472CB00004B/1373